Democratic Realism

Democratic Realism

An American Foreign Policy for a Unipolar World

Charles Krauthammer

The AEI Press

Publisher for the American Enterprise Institute

WASHINGTON, D.C.

2004

Distributed to the Trade by National Book Network, 15200 NBN Way, Blue Ridge Summit, PA 17214. To order call toll free 1-800-462-6420 or 1-717-794-3800. For all other inquiries please contact the AEI Press, 1150 Seventeenth Street, N.W., Washington, D.C. 20036 or call 1-800-862-5801.

American Enterprise Institute
1150 17th Street, N.W.
Washington, D.C. 20036

Printed in the United States of America

Democratic Realism
An American Foreign Policy for a Unipolar World

A Unipolar World

Americans have a healthy aversion to foreign policy. It stems from a sense of thrift: Who needs it? We're protected by two great oceans. We have this continent practically to ourselves. And we share it with just two neighbors, both friendly, one so friendly that its people seem intent upon moving in with us.

It took three giants of the twentieth century to drag us into its great battles: Wilson into World War I, Roosevelt into World War II, Truman into the Cold War. And then it ended with one of the great anticlimaxes in history. Without a shot fired, without a revolution, without so much as a press release, the Soviet Union simply gave up and disappeared.

It was the end of everything—the end of communism, of socialism, of the Cold War, of the European wars. But the end of everything was also a beginning. On December 26, 1991, the Soviet Union died and something new was born, something utterly new—a unipolar world dominated by a single superpower unchecked by any rival and with decisive reach in every corner of the globe.

This is a staggering new development in history, not seen since the fall of Rome. It is so new, so strange, that we have no idea how to deal with it. Our first reaction—the 1990s—was utter confusion. The next reaction was awe. When Paul Kennedy, who had once popularized the idea of American decline, saw what America did in the Afghan war—a display of fully mobilized, furiously concentrated unipolar power at a distance of 8,000 miles—he not only recanted, he stood in wonder: "Nothing has ever existed like this disparity of power," he wrote, "nothing. . . . No other nation comes close. . . . Charlemagne's empire was merely western European in its reach. The Roman empire stretched farther afield, but there was another great empire in Persia, and a larger one in China. There is, therefore, no comparison."

Even Rome is no model for what America is today. First, because we do not have the imperial culture of Rome. We are an Athenian republic, even more republican and infinitely more democratic than Athens. And this American Republic has acquired the largest seeming empire in the history of the world— acquired it in a fit of absent-mindedness greater even than Britain's. And it was not just absent-mindedness; it was sheer inadvertence. We got here because of Europe's suicide in the world wars of the twentieth century, and then the death of its Eurasian successor, Soviet Russia, for having adopted a political and economic system so inhuman that, like a genetically defective organism, it simply expired in its sleep. Leaving us with global dominion.

Second, we are unlike Rome, unlike Britain and France and Spain and the other classical empires of modern times, in that *we do not hunger for territory.* The use of the word "empire" in the American context is ridiculous. It is absurd to apply the word to a people whose first instinct upon arriving on anyone's soil is to demand an exit strategy. I can assure you that when the Romans went into Gaul and the British into India, they were not looking for exit strategies. They were looking for entry strategies.

In David Lean's *Lawrence of Arabia,* King Faisal says to Lawrence: "I think you are another of these desert-loving English. . . . The English have a great hunger for desolate places." Indeed, for five centuries, the Europeans did hunger for deserts and jungles and oceans and new continents.

Americans do not. We like it here. We like our McDonald's. We like our football. We like our rock-and-roll. We've got the Grand Canyon and Graceland. We've got Silicon Valley and South Beach. We've got everything. And if that's not enough, we've got Vegas—

which is a facsimile of everything. What could we possibly need anywhere else? We don't like exotic climates. We don't like exotic languages—lots of declensions and moods. We don't even know what a mood is. We like Iowa corn and New York hot dogs, and if we want Chinese or Indian or Italian, we go to the food court. We don't send the Marines for takeout.

That's because we are not an imperial power. We are a commercial republic. We don't take food; we trade for it. Which makes us something unique in history, an anomaly, a hybrid: a commercial republic with overwhelming global power. A commercial republic that, by pure accident of history, has been designated custodian of the international system. The eyes of every supplicant from East Timor to Afghanistan, from Iraq to Liberia; Arab and Israeli, Irish and British, North and South Korean are upon us.

That is who we are. That is where we are.

Now the question is: What do we do? What is a unipolar power to do?

Isolationism

The oldest and most venerable answer is to hoard that power and retreat. This is known as isolationism. Of all the foreign policy schools in America, it has the oldest pedigree, not surprising in the only great power in history to be isolated by two vast oceans.

Isolationism originally sprang from a view of America as spiritually superior to the Old World. We were too good to be corrupted by its low intrigues, entangled by its cynical alliances.

Today, however, isolationism is an ideology of fear. Fear of trade. Fear of immigrants. Fear of the Other. Isolationists want to cut off trade and immigration, and withdraw from our military and strategic commitments around the world. Even isolationists, of course, did not oppose the war in Afghanistan, because it was so obviously an act of self-defense—only a fool or a knave or a Susan Sontag could oppose that. But anything beyond that, isolationists oppose.

They are for a radical retrenchment of American power—for pulling up the drawbridge to Fortress America.

Isolationism is an important school of thought historically, but not today. Not just because of its brutal intellectual reductionism, but because it is so obviously inappropriate to the world of today—a world of export-driven economies, of massive population flows, and of 9/11, the definitive demonstration that the combination of modern technology and transnational primitivism has erased the barrier between "over there" and over here.

Classical isolationism is not just intellectually obsolete; it is politically bankrupt as well. Four years ago, its most public advocate, Pat Buchanan, ran for president of the United States, and carried Palm Beach. By accident.

Classic isolationism is moribund and marginalized. Who then rules America?

Liberal Internationalism

In the 1990s, it was liberal internationalism. Liberal internationalism is the foreign policy of the Democratic Party and the religion of the foreign policy elite. It has a peculiar history. It traces its pedigree to Woodrow Wilson's utopianism, Harry Truman's anticommunism, and John Kennedy's militant universalism. But after the Vietnam War, it was transmuted into an ideology of passivity, acquiescence and almost reflexive anti-interventionism.

Liberals today proudly take credit for Truman's and Kennedy's roles in containing communism, but they prefer to forget that, for the last half of the Cold War, liberals used "cold warrior" as an epithet. In the early 1980s, they gave us the nuclear freeze movement, a form of unilateral disarmament in the face of Soviet nuclear advances. Today, John Kerry boasts of opposing, during the 1980s, what he calls Ronald Reagan's "illegal war in Central America"—and oppose he did what was, in fact, an indigenous anticommunist rebellion that ultimately succeeded in bringing down Sandinista rule and ushering in democracy in all of Central America.

That boast reminds us how militant was liberal passivity in the last half of the Cold War. But that passivity outlived the Cold War. When Kuwait was invaded, the question was: Should the United States go to war to prevent the Persian Gulf from falling into hostile hands? The Democratic Party joined the Buchananite isolationists in saying No. The Democrats voted No overwhelmingly—two to one in the House, more than four to one in the Senate.

And yet, quite astonishingly, when liberal internationalism came to power just two years later in the form of the Clinton administration, it turned almost hyperinterventionist. It involved us four times in military action: deepening intervention in Somalia, invading Haiti, bombing Bosnia, and finally going to war over Kosovo.

How to explain the amazing transmutation of Cold War and Gulf War doves into Haiti and Balkan hawks? The crucial and obvious difference is this: Haiti, Bosnia and Kosovo were humanitarian ventures—fights for right and good, *devoid of raw national interest*. And only humanitarian interventionism—disinterested interventionism devoid of national interest—is morally pristine enough to justify the use of force. The history of the 1990s refutes the lazy notion that liberals have an aversion to the use of force. They do not. They have an aversion to using force for reasons of pure national interest.

And by national interest I do not mean simple self-defense. Everyone believes in self-defense, as in Afghanistan. I am talking about national interest as defined by a Great Power: shaping the international environment by projecting power abroad to secure economic, political, and strategic goods. Intervening militarily for *that* kind of national interest, liberal internationalism finds unholy and unsupportable. It sees that kind of national interest as merely self-interest writ large, in effect, a form of grand national selfishness. Hence Kuwait, no; Kosovo, yes.

The other defining feature of the Clinton foreign policy was multilateralism, which expressed itself in a mania for treaties. The Clinton administration negotiated a dizzying succession of parchment promises on bioweapons, chemical weapons, nuclear testing, carbon emissions, antiballistic missiles, etc.

Why? No sentient being could believe that, say, the chemical or biological weapons treaties were anything more than transparently useless. Senator Joseph Biden once defended the Chemical Weapons Convention, which even its proponents admitted was unenforceable, on the grounds that it would "provide us with a valuable tool"—the "moral suasion of the entire international community."

Moral suasion? Was it moral suasion that made Qaddafi see the wisdom of giving up his weapons of mass destruction? Or Iran agree for the first time to spot nuclear inspections? It was the suasion of the bayonet. It was the ignominious fall of Saddam—and the desire of interested spectators not to be next on the list. The whole point of this treaty was to keep *rogue states* from developing chemical weapons. Rogue states are, by definition, impervious to moral suasion.

Moral suasion is a farce. Why then this obsession with conventions, protocols, legalisms? Their obvious net effect is to temper American power. Who, after all, was really going to be most constrained by these treaties? The ABM amendments were aimed squarely at American advances and strategic defenses, not at Russia, which lags hopelessly behind. The Kyoto Protocol exempted India and China. The nuclear test ban would have seriously degraded the American nuclear arsenal. And the land mine treaty (which the Clinton administration spent months negotiating but, in the end, met so much Pentagon resistance that even Clinton could not initial it) would have had a devastating impact on U.S. conventional forces, particularly at the DMZ in Korea.

But that, you see, is the whole point of the multilateral enterprise: To reduce American freedom of action by making it subservient to, dependent on, constricted by the will—and interests—of other nations. To tie down Gulliver with a thousand strings. To domesticate the most undomesticated, most outsized, national interest on the planet—ours.

Today, multilateralism remains the overriding theme of liberal internationalism. When in power in the 1990s, multilateralism expressed itself as a mania for treaties. When out of power in this decade, multilateralism manifests itself in the slavish pursuit of "international legitimacy"—and opposition to any American action undertaken without universal foreign blessing.

Which is why the Democratic critique of the war in Iraq is so peculiarly one of process and not of policy. The problem was that we did not have the permission of the UN; we did not have a large enough coalition; we did not have a second Security Council resolution. Kofi Annan was unhappy and the French were cross.

The Democratic presidential candidates all say that we should have internationalized the conflict, brought in the UN, enlisted the allies. Why? Two reasons: assistance and legitimacy. First, they say, we could have used these other countries to help us in the reconstruction.

This is rich. Everyone would like to have more help in reconstruction. It would be lovely to have the Germans and the French helping reconstruct Baghdad. But the question is moot, and the argument is cynical: France and Germany made absolutely clear that they would never support the overthrow of Saddam. So, accommodating them was not a way to get them into the reconstruction, it was a way to ensure that there would never be any reconstruction, because Saddam would still be in power.

Of course it would be nice if we had more allies rather than fewer. It would also be nice to be able to fly. But when some nations are not with you on your enterprise, including them in your coalition is not a way to broaden it; it's a way to abolish it.

At which point, liberal internationalists switch gears and appeal to legitimacy—on the grounds that multilateral action has a higher moral standing. I have always found this line of argument incomprehensible. By what possible moral calculus does an American intervention to liberate 25 million people forfeit moral legitimacy because it lacks the blessing of the butchers of Tiananmen Square or the cynics of the Quai d'Orsay?

Which is why it is hard to take these arguments at face value. Look: We know why liberal internationalists demanded UN sanction for the war in Iraq. It was a way to stop the war. It was the

Gulliver effect. Call a committee meeting of countries with hostile or contrary interests—i.e., the Security Council—and you have guaranteed yourself another twelve years of inaction.

Historically, multilateralism is a way for weak countries to multiply their power by attaching themselves to stronger ones. But multilateralism imposed on Great Powers, and particularly on a unipolar power, is intended to *restrain* that power. Which is precisely why France is an ardent multilateralist. But why should America be?

Why, in the end, *does* liberal internationalism want to tie down Gulliver, to blunt the pursuit of American national interests by making them subordinate to a myriad of other interests?

In the immediate post-Vietnam era, this aversion to national interest might have been attributed to self-doubt and self-loathing. I don't know. What I do know is that today it is a mistake to see liberal foreign policy as deriving from anti-Americanism or lack of patriotism or a late efflorescence of 1960s radicalism.

On the contrary. The liberal aversion to national interest stems from an idealism, a larger vision of country, a vision of some ambition and nobility—the ideal of a true international community. And that is: To transform the international system from the Hobbesian universe into a Lockean universe. To turn the state of nature into a norm-driven community. To turn the law of the jungle into the rule of law—of treaties and contracts and UN resolutions. In short, to remake the international system in the image of domestic civil society.

They dream of a new world, a world described in 1943 by Cordell Hull, FDR's secretary of state—a world in which "there will no longer be need for spheres of influence, for alliances, for balance of power, or any other of the special arrangements by which, in the unhappy past, the nations strove to safeguard their security or promote their interests."

And to create such a true international community, you have to temper, transcend, and, in the end, abolish the very idea of state power and national interest. Hence the antipathy to

American hegemony and American power. If you are going to break the international arena to the mold of domestic society, you have to domesticate its single most powerful actor. You have to abolish American dominance, not only as an affront to fairness, but also as the greatest obstacle on the whole planet to a democratized international system where all live under self-governing international institutions and self-enforcing international norms.

Realism

This vision is all very nice. All very noble. And all very crazy. Which brings us to the third great foreign policy school: realism.

The realist looks at this great liberal project and sees a hopeless illusion. Because turning the Hobbesian world that has existed since long before the Peloponnesian Wars into a Lockean world, turning a jungle into a suburban subdivision, requires a revolution in human nature. Not just an erector set of new institutions, but a revolution in human nature. And realists do not believe in revolutions in human nature, much less stake their future, and the future of their nation, on them.

Realism recognizes the fundamental fallacy in the whole idea of the international system being modeled on domestic society.

First, what holds domestic society together is a supreme central authority wielding a monopoly of power and enforcing norms. In the international arena there is no such thing. Domestic society may look like a place of self-regulating norms, but if somebody breaks into your house, you call 911, and the police arrive with guns drawn. That's not exactly self-enforcement. That's law enforcement.

Second, domestic society rests on the shared goodwill, civility and common values of its individual members. What values are shared by, say, Britain, Cuba, Yemen and Zimbabwe—all nominal members of this fiction we call the "international community"?

Of course, you can have smaller communities of shared interests—NAFTA, ANZUS, or the European Union. But the European conceit that relations with all nations—regardless of ideology, regardless of culture, regardless even of open hostility—should be transacted on the EU model of suasion and norms and negotiations and solemn contractual agreements is an illusion. A fisheries treaty with Canada is something real. An Agreed Framework on plutonium processing with the likes of North Korea is not worth the paper it is written on.

The realist believes the definition of peace Ambrose Bierce offered in *The Devil's Dictionary:* "Peace: *noun,* in international affairs, a period of cheating between two periods of fighting."

Hence the realist axiom: The "international community" is a fiction. It is not a community, it is a cacophony—of straining ambitions, disparate values and contending power.

What does hold the international system together? What keeps it from degenerating into total anarchy? Not the phony security of treaties, not the best of goodwill among the nicer nations. In the unipolar world we inhabit, what stability we do enjoy today is owed to the overwhelming power and deterrent threat of the United States.

If someone invades your house, you call the cops. Who do you call if someone invades your country? You dial Washington. In the unipolar world, the closest thing to a centralized authority, to an enforcer of norms, is America—American power. And ironically, American power is precisely what liberal internationalism wants to constrain and tie down and subsume in pursuit of some brave new Lockean world.

Realists do not live just in America. I found one in Finland. During the 1997 negotiations in Oslo over the land mine treaty, one of the rare holdouts, interestingly enough, was *Finland.* The Finnish prime minister stoutly opposed the land mine ban. And for that he was scolded by his Scandinavian neighbors. To which he responded tartly that this was a "very convenient" pose for the "other Nordic countries"—after all, Finland is their land mine.

Finland is the land mine between Russia and Scandinavia. America is the land mine between barbarism and civilization.

Where would South Korea be without America and its land mines along the DMZ? Where would Europe—with its cozy arrogant community—be had America not saved it from the Soviet colossus? Where would the Middle East be had American power not stopped Saddam in 1991?

The land mine that protects civilization from barbarism is not parchment but power, and in a unipolar world, American power—wielded, if necessary, unilaterally. If necessary, preemptively,

Now, those uneasy with American power have made these two means of wielding it—preemption and unilateralism—the focus of unrelenting criticism. The doctrine of preemption, in particular, has been widely attacked for violating international norms.

What international norm? The one under which Israel was universally condemned—even the Reagan administration joined the condemnation at the Security Council—for preemptively destroying Iraq's Osirak nuclear reactor in 1981? Does anyone today doubt that it was the right thing to do, both strategically and morally?

In a world of terrorists, terrorist states and weapons of mass destruction, the option of preemption is especially necessary. In the bipolar world of the Cold War, with a stable nonsuicidal adversary, deterrence could work. Deterrence does not work against people who ache for heaven. It does not work against *undeterrables*. And it does not work against undetectables: nonsuicidal enemy regimes that might attack through clandestine means—a suitcase nuke or anonymously delivered anthrax. Against both undeterrables and undetectables, preemption is the only possible strategy.

Moreover, the doctrine of preemption against openly hostile states pursuing weapons of mass destruction is an improvement on classical deterrence. Traditionally, we deterred the use of WMDs by the threat of retaliation after we'd been attacked—and that's too late; the point of preemption is to deter the very acquisition of WMDs in the first place.

Whether or not Iraq had large stockpiles of WMDs, the very fact that the United States overthrew a hostile regime that repeatedly refused to come clean on its weapons has had precisely this deterrent effect. We are safer today not just because Saddam is gone, but because Libya and any others contemplating trafficking with WMDs, have—for the first time—seen that it carries a cost, a very high cost.

Yes, of course, imperfect intelligence makes preemption problematic. But that is not an objection on principle, it is an objection in practice. Indeed, the objection concedes the principle. We need good intelligence. But we remain defenseless if we abjure the option of preemption.

The other great objection to the way American unipolar power has been wielded is its unilateralism. I would dispute how unilateralist we have in fact been. Constructing ad hoc "coalitions of the willing" hardly qualifies as unilateralism just because they do not have a secretariat in Brussels or on the East River.

Moreover, unilateralism is often the very road to multilateralism. As we learned from the Gulf War, it is the leadership of the United States—indeed, its willingness to act unilaterally if necessary—that galvanized the Gulf War coalition into existence. Without the president of the United States declaring "This will not stand" about the invasion of Kuwait—and making it clear that America would go it alone if it had to—there never would have been the great wall-to-wall coalition that is now so retroactively applauded and held up as a model of multilateralism.

Of course one acts in concert with others if possible. It is nice when others join us in the breach. No one seeks to be unilateral. Unilateralism simply means that one does not allow oneself to be held hostage to the will of others.

Of course you build coalitions when possible. In 2003, we garnered a coalition of the willing for Iraq that included substantial allies like Britain, Australia, Spain, Italy and much of Eastern Europe. France and Germany made clear from the beginning that they would never join in the overthrow of Saddam. Therefore the choice was not a wide coalition versus a narrow one, but a narrow coalition versus none. There were serious arguments against war in Iraq—but the fact France did not approve was not one of them.

Irving Kristol once explained that he preferred the Organization of American States to the United Nations because in the OAS we can be voted down in only three languages, thereby saving translators' fees. Realists choose not to be Gulliver. In an international system with no sovereign, no police, no protection—where power is the ultimate arbiter and history has bequeathed us unprecedented power—we should be vigilant in preserving that power. And our freedom of action to use it.

But here we come up against the limits of realism: You cannot live by power alone. Realism is a valuable antidote to the woolly internationalism of the 1990s. But realism can only take you so far.

Its basic problem lies in its definition of national interest as classically offered by its great theorist, Hans Morgenthau: interest defined as power. Morgenthau postulated that what drives nations, what motivates their foreign policy, is the will to power—to keep it and expand it.

For most Americans, will to power might be a correct description of the world—of what motivates other countries—but it cannot be a prescription for America. It cannot be our purpose. America cannot and will not live by realpolitik alone. Our foreign policy must be driven by something beyond power. Unless conservatives present ideals to challenge the liberal ideal of a domesticated international community, they will lose the debate.

Which is why among American conservatives, another, more idealistic, school has arisen that sees America's national interest as an expression of values.

Democratic Globalism

It is this fourth school that has guided U.S. foreign policy in this decade. This conservative alternative to realism is often lazily and invidiously called neoconservatism, but that is a very odd name for a school whose major proponents in the world today are George W. Bush and Tony Blair—if they are neoconservatives, then Margaret Thatcher was a liberal. There's nothing neo about Bush, and there's nothing con about Blair.

Yet they are the principal proponents today of what might be called democratic globalism, a foreign policy that defines the national interest not as power but as values, and that identifies one supreme value, what John Kennedy called "the success of liberty." As President Bush put it in his speech at Whitehall last November: "The United States and Great Britain share a mission in the world beyond the balance of power or the simple pursuit of interest. We seek the advance of freedom and the peace that freedom brings."

Beyond power. Beyond interest. Beyond interest defined as power. That is the credo of democratic globalism. Which explains its political appeal: America is a nation uniquely built not on blood, race or consanguinity, but on a proposition—to which its sacred honor has been pledged for two centuries. This American exceptionalism explains why non-Americans find this foreign policy so difficult to credit; why Blair has had more difficulty garnering support for it in his country; and why Europe, in particular, finds this kind of value-driven foreign policy hopelessly and irritatingly moralistic.

Democratic globalism sees as the engine of history not the will to power but the will to freedom. And while it has been attacked as a dreamy, idealistic innovation, its inspiration comes from the Truman Doctrine of 1947, the Kennedy inaugural of 1961, and Reagan's "evil empire" speech of 1983. They all sought to recast a struggle for power between two geopolitical titans into a struggle between freedom and unfreedom, and yes, good and evil.

Which is why the Truman Doctrine was heavily criticized by realists like Hans Morgenthau and George Kennan—and Reagan was vilified by the entire foreign policy establishment: for the sin of ideologizing the Cold War by injecting a moral overlay.

That was then. Today, post-9/11, we find ourselves in a similar existential struggle but with a different enemy: not Soviet communism, but Arab-Islamic totalitarianism, both secular and religious. Bush and Blair are similarly attacked for naively and crudely casting this struggle as one of freedom versus unfreedom, good versus evil.

Now, given the way not just freedom but human decency were suppressed in both Afghanistan and Iraq, the two major battles of this new war, you would have to give Bush and Blair's moral claims the decided advantage of being obviously true.

Nonetheless, something can be true and still be dangerous. Many people are deeply uneasy with the Bush-Blair doctrine—many conservatives in particular. When Blair declares in his address to Congress: "The spread of freedom is . . . our last line of defense and our first line of attack," they see a dangerously expansive, aggressively utopian foreign policy. In short, they see Woodrow Wilson.

Now, to a conservative, Woodrow Wilson is fightin' words. Yes, this vision is expansive and perhaps utopian. But it ain't Wilsonian. Wilson envisioned the spread of democratic values through as-yet-to-be invented international institutions. He could be forgiven for that. In 1918, there was no way to know how utterly corrupt and useless those international institutions would turn out to be. Eight decades of bitter experience later—with Libya chairing the UN Commission on Human Rights—there is no way *not* to know.

Democratic globalism is not Wilsonian. Its attractiveness is precisely that it shares realism's insights about the centrality of power. Its attractiveness is precisely that it has appropriate contempt for the fictional legalisms of liberal internationalism.

Moreover, democratic globalism is an improvement over realism. What it can teach realism is that the spread of democracy is not just an end but a means, an indispensable means for securing American interests. The reason is simple. Democracies are inherently more friendly to the United States, less belligerent to their neighbors, and generally more inclined to peace. Realists are right that to protect your interests you often have to go around the world bashing bad guys over the head. But that technique, no matter how satisfying, has its limits. At some point, you have to implant something, something organic and self-developing. And that something is democracy.

But where? The danger of democratic globalism is its universalism, its open-ended commitment to human freedom, its temptation to plant the flag of democracy everywhere. It must learn to say no. And indeed, it does say no. But when it says no to Liberia, or Congo, or Burma, or countenances alliances with authoritarian rulers in places like Pakistan or, for that matter, Russia, it stands accused of hypocrisy. Which is why we must articulate criteria for saying yes.

Where to intervene? Where to bring democracy? Where to nation-build? I propose a single criterion: where it counts.

Call it democratic *realism*. And this is its axiom: *We will support democracy everywhere, but we will commit blood and treasure only in places where there is a strategic necessity—meaning, places central to the larger war against the existential enemy, the enemy that poses a global mortal threat to freedom.*

Where does it count? Fifty years ago, Germany and Japan counted. Why? Because they were the seeds of the greatest global threat to freedom in midcentury—fascism—and then were turned, by nation building, into bulwarks against the next great threat to freedom, Soviet communism.

Where does it count today? Where the overthrow of radicalism and the beginnings of democracy can have a decisive effect in the war against the new global threat to freedom, the new existential enemy, the Arab-Islamic totalitarianism that has threatened us in both its secular and religious forms for the quarter-century since the Khomeini revolution of 1979.

Establishing civilized, decent, nonbelligerent, pro-Western polities in Afghanistan and Iraq and ultimately their key neighbors would, like the flipping of Germany and Japan in the 1940s, change the strategic balance in the fight against Arab-Islamic radicalism.

Yes, it may be a bridge too far. Realists have been warning against the hubris of thinking we can transform an alien culture because of some postulated natural and universal human will to freedom. And they may yet be right. But how do they know in advance? Half a century ago, we heard the same confident warnings about the imperviousness to democracy of Confucian culture. That proved stunningly wrong. Where is it written that Arabs are incapable of democracy?

Yes, as in Germany and Japan, the undertaking is enormous, ambitious and arrogant. It may yet fail. But we cannot afford not to try. There is not a single, remotely plausible, alternative strategy for attacking the monster behind 9/11. It's not Osama bin Laden; it is the cauldron of political oppression, religious intolerance, and social ruin in the Arab-Islamic world—oppression transmuted and deflected by regimes with no legitimacy into virulent, murderous anti-Americanism. It's not one man; it is a condition. It will be nice to find that man and hang him, but that's the cops-and-robbers law-enforcement model of fighting terrorism that we tried for twenty years and that gave us 9/11. This is war, and in war arresting murderers is nice. But you win by taking territory—and leaving something behind.

September 11

We are the unipolar power and what do we do?

In August 1900, David Hilbert gave a speech to the International Congress of Mathematicians naming twenty-three still-unsolved mathematical problems bequeathed by the nineteenth century to the twentieth. Had he presented the great unsolved geopolitical problems bequeathed to the twentieth century, one would have stood out above all—the rise of Germany and its accommodation within the European state system.

Similarly today, at the dawn of the twenty-first century, we can see clearly the two great geopolitical challenges on the horizon: the inexorable rise of China and the coming demographic collapse of Europe, both of which will irrevocably disequilibrate the international system.

But those problems come later. They are for midcentury. They are for the next generation. And that generation will not even get to these problems unless we first deal with our problem.

And our problem is 9/11 and the roots of Arab-Islamic nihilism. September 11 felt like a new problem, but for all its shock and surprise, it is an old problem with a new face. September 11 felt like the initiation of a new history, but it was a return to history, the twentieth-century history of radical ideologies and existential enemies.

The anomaly is not the world of today. The anomaly was the 1990s, our holiday from history. It felt like peace, but it was an interval of dreaming between two periods of reality.

From which 9/11 awoke us. It startled us into thinking everything was new. It's not. What is new is what happened not on 9/11 but ten years earlier on December 26, 1991: the emergence of the United States as the world's unipolar power. What is unique is our advantage in this struggle, an advantage we did not have during the struggles of the twentieth century. The question for our time is how to press this advantage, how to exploit our unipolar power, how to deploy it to win the old/new war that exploded upon us on 9/11.

What is the unipolar power to do?

Four schools, four answers.

The isolationists want simply to ignore unipolarity, pull up the drawbridge, and defend Fortress America. Alas, the Fortress has no moat—not after the airplane, the submarine, the ballistic missile—and as for the drawbridge, it was blown up on 9/11.

Then there are the liberal internationalists. They like to dream, and to the extent they are aware of our unipolar power, they don't like it. They see its use for anything other than humanitarianism or reflexive self-defense as an expression of national selfishness. And they don't just want us to ignore our unique power, they want us to yield it piece by piece, by subsuming ourselves in a new global architecture in which America becomes not the arbiter of international events, but a good and tame international citizen.

Then there is realism, which has the clearest understanding of the new unipolarity and its uses—unilateral and preemptive if necessary. But in the end, it fails because it offers no vision. It is all means and no ends. It cannot adequately define our mission.

Hence, the fourth school: democratic globalism. It has, in this decade, rallied the American people to a struggle over values. It seeks to vindicate the American idea by making the spread of democracy, the success of liberty, the ends and means of American foreign policy.

I support that. I applaud that. But I believe it must be tempered in its universalistic aspirations and rhetoric from a democratic globalism to a democratic realism. It must be targeted, focused and limited. We are friends to all, but we come ashore only where it really counts. And where it counts today is that Islamic crescent stretching from North Africa to Afghanistan.

In October 1962, during the Cuban Missile Crisis, we came to the edge of the abyss. Then, accompanied by our equally shaken adversary, we both deliberately drew back. On September 11, 2001, we saw the face of Armageddon again, but this time with an enemy that does not draw back. This time the enemy knows no reason.

Were that the only difference between now and then, our situation would be hopeless. But there is a second difference between now and then: the uniqueness of our power, unrivaled, not just today but ever. That evens the odds. The rationality of the enemy is something beyond our control. But the use of our power is within our control. And if that power is used wisely, constrained not by illusions and fictions but only by the limits of our mission—which is to bring a modicum of freedom as an antidote to nihilism—we can prevail.

About the Author

Charles Krauthammer is an essayist and syndicated columnist. His *Washington Post* column appears in more than 130 newspapers worldwide. He writes a monthly essay for *Time* magazine and contributes frequently to *The Weekly Standard*, *The New Republic*, *The National Interest* and other journals. His columns have been awarded the Pulitzer Prize for distinguished commentary; his essays, the National Magazine Award for essays and criticism. He is the recipient of the Bradley Prize for promotion of liberal democracy and American institutions, and, on the occasion of the presentation of this essay, the American Enterprise Institute's highest honor, the Irving Kristol Award.